Erling Bisgaard · Gulle Stehouwer

MUSICBOOK O

PULSE • PITCH
RHYTHM • FORM
DYNAMICS

SONGS • GAMES
MOVEMENT ACTIVITIES
FOR TEACHING MUSIC
TO YOUNG CHILDREN

EDITED AND ADAPTED BY
TOSSI AARON

© Magnamusic/Edition Wilhelm Hansen, U.S.A. 1976

St. Louis, MO 63132

CONTENTS

ISBN 0-918812-04-6

MUSICBOOK O

Musicbook O offers teachers an interesting variety of activities for music education in kindergarten and the early grades.

AIM:
To introduce the fundamentals of music through singing, movement and simple games. The young child's developing social awareness can be encouraged as the class works on a common task. His coordination and concentration can grow as he participates fully in these natural, joyful group activities.

CONTENTS:
Most of the exercises have been adapted from traditional folk materials to suit the aims mentioned above. Each section accents one of the basic concepts of music: pulse, sound/silence, dynamics, pitch, rhythm and form.

USE:
The particular progression of these sections need not be followed exactly. To the contrary, every teacher should seek and find a suitable sequence based on the conditions of the individual situation or the concepts to be taught. For example, a new game may be effectively introduced when it begins in the same formation as the one just ended.

The frequency and duration of each activity is up to the teacher, based on accurate observation of the children's response to the game and each other. Because young children learn best by imitation, the wise teacher will participate in all the games on equal terms with the class. Any of the simple instrumental parts may be relegated to the children as soon as they have developed sufficient rhythmic security. Every child should be encouraged to try.

For some games, visual aids may prove useful and effective. The drawings in *Musicbook O* may be duplicated on the blackboard, on individual worksheets, or traced onto transparencies for use in an overhead projector.

This book was not intended as a complete curriculum outline. It is hoped that it will be used as a source book of ideas, stimulating teachers to collect, adapt and improvise similar materials suitable for their classes. In this way, a most important aspect of early education will find a place in the lives of young children: singing and singing games.

The authors wish to thank the American Editor, Tossi Aaron, for folklore research and the writing of singable English words for the songs. We gratefully acknowledge her helpful suggestions and revisions that made this English edition possible.

Erling Bisgaard
Gulle Stehouwer

Introduction to the American Edition

Erling Bisgaard and Gulle Stehouwer are leading music educators in Denmark, the former at university level and the latter as art and music teacher in the intermediate grades. In addition, Mr. Bisgaard conducts a leading choir and orchestra. Mrs. Stehouwer drew the illustrations and did the layout for this book. Together they have given many workshops in Scandinavia, and have prepared a graded series of materials for music education in Danish schools. These consist of teacher's books and student workbooks. *Musicbook O,* under the same title in Danish, is the first to appear in English and in the United States.

Teachers will find the songs and games imaginative and appealing, the concepts clearly and directly presented and the whole collection immediately useful. With a little ingenuity, all the games can be pruned to fit the limitations of space and time that beset the typical classroom teacher in the early grades. The title page of each chapter has been designed to allow space for your additions, notes and new inventions.

Unless otherwise specified, all the melodies and games are based on Scandinavian folklore and have close relatives in the United States. Where I have made editorial suggestions or added supplementary material, it has come out of direct experience with the games in my own music classes, extending over one school year. In some cases, the children themselves, in grades K-3, have made unconscious revisions.

They soon selected their favorite games, and asked for them often, proving that the roots of children's play reach all over the world, and that this transplant from Scandinavia can grow and flower in American classrooms and wherever English is spoken.

May, 1976   *Tossi Aaron*

FORMATIONS

SCATTERED
CIRCLE
SNAKE
PARTNERS,
etc.

5

To clarify and simplify the games in this book, and to enable the teacher to gain a rapid impression of the formation needed, a diagram will be found next to each game described. A complete key to these diagrams will be found on page 74.

Scattered formation, stationary

The children are dispersed evenly over the entire floor area, each in his "own space", with room to move, yet not interfering with his neighbor's space. Adjustments can be made for sitting, legs folded, or lying flat.

Scattered, moving

Example: A small sound, perhaps a finger snap, signals the class to begin to move around the room. A second signal indicates a complete stop, and the children check to see that they are all evenly spaced in the area.

Variation: This exercise is explored using various combinations of movement patterns — forward, backward, on tiptoe, arms up, close to the floor, etc. This all is done without meter, letting the class find its own way as individuals, but with regard for others' way of moving.

At the Bottom of the Sea

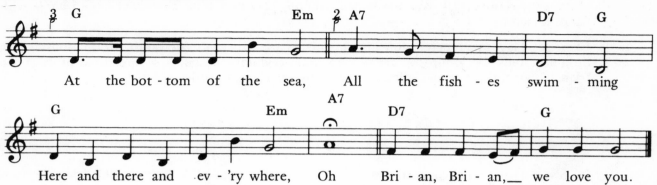

At the bot - tom of the sea, All the fish - es swim - ming

Here and there and ev - 'ry where, Oh Bri - an, Bri - an,__ we love you.

Formation: Scattered, all seated but one; eventually, short lines. The seated children wave arms and bodies like aquatic plants, and begin the game by singing to the solo child by name, "Linda, Linda, we love you." Linda runs lightly among her classmates as the song begins again. At the word "Oh . . ." she stops in front of another child, and the class sings his name: "Brian, Brian, we love you." Brian stands, steps in front of Linda, and becomes the new leader, determing where to stop the next time around. When the length of the line becomes cumbersome, divide into two or three shorter lines, each with a leader.

The Birthday Party

La la La la La la La la La la La la la La La la La la La la La.
When Su -san-na has a hap-py birth-day par - ty, e -ven Pe -ter wants to come a - long.

Formation: Scattered, all seated but one; eventually, short lines. Begin with the "la la" as the solo child runs lightly among the class. On the last note, she stops in front of someone, and both of their names are inserted in the song, as shown above. The new child becomes the leader. The class claps the pulse during the "la la" singing.

Circle

The ring formation is the most useful as well as the most ancient group shape. Facing into the center, seated or standing, allows each person to see all the others, and promotes a feeling of unity and security. All over the world children play and their elders dance in a circle with hands joined.

Exercise: Play small percussion instruments as sound signals for various formations: *e.g.* a drumbeat tells the group to form a circle, a woodblock signals a square. Find others for a triangle shape, three small circles, etc. The children can take turns directing.

Snake

By breaking the circle at one place, the more flexible "snake" is formed. Children take turns at being the "head" and determining the direction of movement. After he has had his turn, the leader moves to the end of the snake and becomes the "tail", thus learning to be both leader and follower.

Exercise: The head determines the floor pattern of the snake: straight lines, zig-zag, spiral, etc.

Variation: The head determines how the line moves: stamping, hopping, sliding, skipping. This is done as in "Follow the Leader", without meter or drumbeat, or piano, but rather for its own sake.

Small snakes

The large snake divides at several points, forming short lines of five or six children in each. The head of every snake is responsible for keeping his line moving in a random use of the entire space, without touching, colliding or otherwise interfering with any other snake.

Exercise: Change leaders in the same way as with the single snake, perhaps playing a single beat on a triangle as a signal. Have the leaders determine direction and manner of moving.

Turn the Ring Around

Turn and turn the ring a-round, Un - til a Queen or King is found. For

Han-nah we will curt-sy, For Han-nah we will bow, For Han-nah, she must turn a-round.

Possible accompaniment for alto xylophone, played initially by the teacher and eventually by the children.

 etc.

Circle, holding hands, with one child in the center.

During the first phrase, the circle walks slowly to the right (counter-clockwise), while the center child walks in the opposite direction. Both stop at *, inserting the name of the child directly in front of the center child at that moment. All follow the actions of the song, curtsy-ing and bowing to the chosen one. On the last few words, "Hannah" turns to face outward, releasing hands, and rejoining them by the last word. The game may be ended at any time, or when all (in a small group) are facing outward, by singing a last verse of . .* "For we all like to curtsy, for we all like to turn around" at which point the whole circle turns to face the center again.

Every two or three turns, change the center child by having one of the "chosen ones" come into the center. Children enjoy playing triangle or finger cymbals on the accent.

**Pair
formation**

Partner exercises are among the most demanding, and at the same time, most valuable social contact exercises. As with the "snake" formations, they help to develop self-confidence and the ability to lead as well as follow. Working in pairs is essential in the early stages. It encourages children's acceptance of their own and others' performance and builds improvisational abilities in rhythm, melody and movement.

**Partners in
scattered
formation**

Exercise: "Find a partner". One of the pair is a leader, and holds out his hands, palms upward. The other child places his fingers very lightly on the leader's palms, closes his eyes, and allows himself to be led slowly around the room by this very small contact. The leader, moving at random in the given space, must ensure that there are no collisions. On a predetermined sound signal (wood block, triangle), the roles (and eventually, the partners) are exchanged.

**Partners in a
circle, or a
double circle**

"We'll form pairs in a circle" or "Make a circle of partners".
This formation is the starting point for many singing games and dance-songs. Partners can face counter-clockwise, clockwise, or be in two circles moving in opposite directions. Partners can stay together throughout the song or move up to a new partner at certain specified times.
Examples: Page 29, Page 33.

SOUND/SILENCE

LISTENING
REACTION TO SOUND AND SILENCE
DISTINGUISHING BETWEEN VARIOUS SOUNDS
SELECTION AND COMBINATION OF SOUNDS

— to listen actively
— to be able to distinguish between varied sounds
— to be able to describe different sounds
— to experiment with using these sounds in various ways

The class sits anywhere in the room, eyes closed and covered. When the teacher strikes one beat on a percussion instrument, they point toward the source of the sound, keeping their eyes closed. When the teacher says "look", they open their eyes and check to see if they were correct. Eyes are closed again, and the teacher (subsequently a child), creeps silently to another place in the room to begin again.

Suggestion: Introduce a bit of fantasy by telling the class that an Indian in soft moccasins is walking in the woods and suddenly steps on a twig and cracks it. (Use claves to make the short, sharp sound.) All the animals in the forest hear it and turn their heads (point) to the sound.

Scattered formation, eyes closed. The teacher strikes an instrument whose sound is of long duration, such as a triangle or hanging cymbal. The children move in any way they choose, as long as the sound is audible. When it has faded away or the teacher damps the sound with her hand, all movement ceases. This may be done from sitting, standing in place and/or moving in slow motion.

The children run lightly in random formation while the teacher plays rapid, continuous sounds on a tambourine, jingle sticks, maracas or castanets. The children "freeze" when the sounds stop, and wait for a repeat. This may also be done using piano, recorder or a song being sung.

Variation: Reverse this and have the children move at random in the silence, and stop when there is sound.

The Robbers

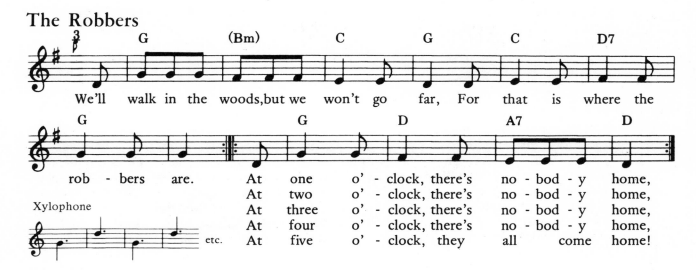

We'll walk in the woods, but we won't go far, For that is where the
rob - bers are.

At one o' - clock, there's no - bod - y home,
At two o' - clock, there's no - bod - y home,
At three o' - clock, there's no - bod - y home,
At four o' - clock, there's no - bod - y home,
At five o' - clock, they all come home!

Xylophone
etc.

Four or five children are chosen to be the first "trees in the woods". They secretly decide which ones will be camouflaged robbers, or robbers hiding behind trees. Then they take up positions anywhere in the room, and stand with arms upraised like branches. The rest of the players stroll among the trees, singing the song. On the last word of the song ("home"), the disguised robbers capture anyone near them, and these become trees, too. Each time the group goes off and decides which of them will be robbers, and which will remain placid trees. Eventually all the children will be caught, and the game ends.

Instrumentation Five children can be selected to play instruments (*e.g.,* triangle, finger cymbals, cymbal), one at the end of each "hour" mentioned in the second part of the song: Either

At one o'clock there's nobody home ♩ (first child)

At two o'clock there's nobody home ♩ ♩ (second child, etc.), or each child plays only his own stroke, cumulatively.

Or, only the five o'clock is played, one stroke by each instrument, and the robbers make their catch on the last sound.

Reaction to sound Variation: One child, or the teacher, plays the clock chimes as the whole group "freezes" in place at the end of each line. "At three o'clock there's nobody home" . . . (freeze) ♩ ♩ ♩

After some experience, or with slightly older children, certain adaptations may evolve. As the group becomes geometrically increased, each tree may decide for himself whether or not to be a robber <u>this</u> time. Robbers in disguise may need reminding to stand very still and not run after their quarry, but only grab who is nearest.

Two or three spaces are clearly outlined on the floor, using a few yards of string or chalk marks. As the teacher plays a drum or a melody instrument, the children move at random outside these spaces. When the sound ends, they move rapidly into one of the marked areas, and hold their position in silence until the sounds begin anew.

Choose two different sounding percussion instruments, perhaps a drum and a triangle. The class moves at random, quietly and without accompaniment. The teacher plays one beat on the drum, and the children lie down quickly. Pause until all is silent. At a stroke on the triangle, the children rise and move again at their own pace. While the children are lying on the floor, the teacher can walk around quietly, checking to see if all the "rag dolls" are asleep (completely relaxed), by lifting an arm or a leg and seeing that it falls very limply back to the floor. Commend those who are really good at "rag doll sleeping" (all!) with a little pat.

The teacher signals with one drum beat for the class to walk forward (in random movement) and with two beats for a change to backward. Pupils can take turns direction.

Variation: Several new signals can be added: a triangle stroke to stand still, a wood block to stoop down, etc. Add signals carefully, one at a time, as the children increase their ability to remember them.

Small circles

Several small circles, each with a large ball or beanbag, easy to catch. The ball is passed around the circle until the teacher gives a sound cue for a change of direction.

Someone Special Gets the Drum

Lis-ten, lis-ten, here I come, some-one spe-cial gets the drum.

Melody: Orff-Schulwerk Vol. I
© B. Schott's Sons
used by permission

Possible Xylophone Part

Form

The children move at random while the song is sung twice. By the last word, they try to be standing in a circle, with eyes closed. (This requires considerable judgment on their part, and may need some practice.)

Listening

The teacher (next a child) walks around the outside of the circle, tapping the drum. Stopping behind someone, he also stops the drum. As soon as a child becomes aware that the drum has stopped behind him, he turns, takes the drum, and plays one strong beat as a signal for the song and the random walking to begin again.

Younger children or those in a large class can remain in scattered positions, just standing still with eyes closed when the song ends.

Short lines of five or six children in "snake" formation. On a signal from an instrument, perhaps a cymbal, the lines move at random, each following its leader. On a second signal, perhaps a woodblock, the "head" goes to the end of the line and becomes the "tail". The leader determines where the line goes, and is responsible for using the whole space equally, without collisions or "traffic jams".

Variation: The leader may also determine the manner of moving, such as large steps, tiptoe, hopping, creeping, or skipping.

The class sits or lies relaxed, with eyes closed, evenly spread out on the floor. In complete stillness, they listen to the sounds of their environment. After a full minute or even two, let each try to tell what sounds were heard; footsteps in the hall, a dog barking or cars outside, even their own heartbeats. In this way, their attention is drawn to sounds they do not normally isolate. An assignment to collect and remember sounds at home or on the way to school can be listed by the teacher, and recalled later in other games and dramatic play.

The class sits in a semi-circle, eyes closed. The teacher makes two consecutive, casually related sounds: knock, then open the door; sneeze, blow nose, etc. The children open their eyes and try to guess and/or imitate what they heard in the same order. Extend the exercise; include three sounds. Eventually the children can take turns producing the sounds. Whoever reproduces or names the sounds in correct order gets the next turn.

I Lost My Ring

I lost my ring when it slipped off my fin-ger, the ding-a-ling

ring-er, Please help me find it, oh where is my ring?

(Will I find it?)

Reaction to sound

Singing

Listening

Two children are chosen, one as "seeker" the other as "hider," who carries sleighbells.

The whole group moves at random and in silence, using the whole space. At a sound signal from the teacher, such as a triangle stroke, a circle is formed with the seeker inside and the hider outside. Those standing in the circle put their hands behind their backs. The seeker closes or covers his eyes. As the song is sung, the hider, keeping the bells as quiet as possible, walks around the outside of the circle, and places the bells into a pair of waiting hands.

By the end of the song, the hider joins the circle, the seeker opens his eyes, and all those in the circle jiggle their hands as if they have the bells behind them. The seeker must then judge aurally where the bells are. If he can correctly name who has them, he takes the bells and becomes the hider, while the child who had them becomes the seeker. Should he guess incorrectly, he is seeker again and the recipient is hider. Begin again in silent, random motion.

With eyes closed, the class sits in a semi-circle on the floor. The teacher makes a sound with hands, feet or mouth, such as a snap, brush hands together, tongue click, whisper, foot tap, etc. Opening their eyes, individual children try to name and/or imitate the sound. Eventually, they can do this for each other. Extend by making several sounds in a row.

Variation: Use sounds made with objects in the room; turn pages in a book, open a drawer, roll a pencil, pull the shade.

The children listen to, and learn the names of several small percussion instruments played by themselves or the teacher. Once these are familiar, the children close their eyes, and the teacher tiptoes over and plays one of them, briefly.

"Who can say the name of the instrument you heard?"
"Who can say the name and come play it?"

A number of familiar-sounding percussion instruments are placed in the center of a seated circle. The teacher, with duplicates of a few of them, goes out of sight of the class behind a door or the piano, and strikes two of the instruments in sequence. Individual children try to reproduce what they heard in the same sequence. The one who imitates correctly may be the next to play out of sight.

Eventually the game can and should be extended to three sounds.

Three Small Musicians

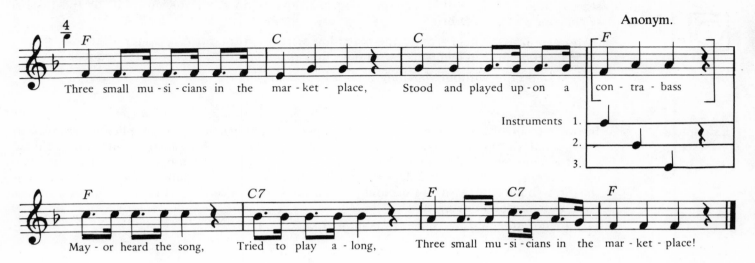

Anonym.

Three small mu - si - cians in the mar - ket - place, Stood and played up - on a con - tra - bass

May - or heard the song, Tried to play a - long, Three small mu - si - cians in the mar - ket - place!

listening

After the children know the song well, ask them to try singing it and then keeping silent on the word "contrabass". Practice this internalizing, perhaps by having them tap those three beats with one finger: "sing that word in your head". When this is secure, three children, each with a different small percussion instrument, conceal themselves out of sight behind a door or the piano. The class sings the song, keeping silent on "contrabass" while the three instruments are heard in sequence instead. (The instrumentalists have secretly agreed among themselves the order in which they will play.) The other children try to remember the exact sequence heard.

Variation: Change the words of the third phrase to "Conductor heard the song". Have one child be the conductor and then conduct the three instruments in proper order.

If needed, the class can practice the three beats with soft claps. Divide the class into three groups, each playing one of the beats in sequence; the instrumentalists might be chosen from among several trial trios that work well together.

This game may be co-ordinated with a lesson or demonstration on the double bass, as part of the string family.

Example A

Drawings of familiar percussion instruments are put on the board. In the center of a circle of seated children, place the corresponding instruments on the floor. A child, or the teacher selects one and plays it briefly.

"Who can draw a circle around the matching picture on the board?" Later a series of two or three instruments can be played, with one child at the board pointing out the sequence.

"Who can do this without watching what is happening?"

Example B

In order to involve the whole class in active listening and participation, duplicate a sheet of instrument drawings for each child. The teacher plays two or three instruments consecutively, and the children number them in sequence. If the children are too young to draw numbers easily, geometric figures or colors can indicate the order of the sounds. "Draw a circle around the first sound and a square around the second." Or, "Color the first instrument you hear red and the second one blue."

Eventually this can be extended to include three sounds.

Example C

As above, instrument drawings are put on the board. This time, the instruments are widely spaced on the floor. The teacher, and later a child, goes for a walk among them, playing three along the way.

"Who can draw a line to show the path I took?"

In the beginning, it will help to put an "X" at the starting point of the walk.

Variation: One child faces the board so he cannot see the walking, but must trace the path solely by aural clues.

Variation: Each child has a sheet of instrument drawings. The teacher (and later a child) takes a few instruments out of sight, and plays a short sequence of three or four of them. The children draw a "walking line" from one to the other as they are played.

Many games can be invented with these sheets.

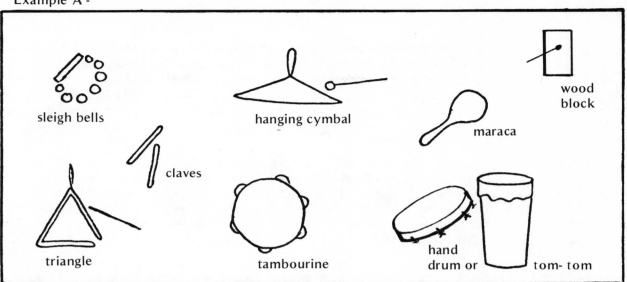

sleigh bells

hanging cymbal

maraca

wood block

claves

triangle

tambourine

hand drum or

tom-tom

Example B -

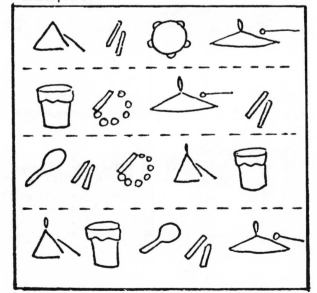

Example C -

Three or four children face away from the class with eyes closed. Two instruments are played in sequence. The first child turns, eyes open, and tries to duplicate the sounds. If he is correct, he gets a silent nod from the teacher, and chooses a third instrument to add to the series. The next child tries in the same way to duplicate the extended series. If there is an error, the next in line tries. Avoid playing similar sounding instruments (wood block, claves) consecutively.

Partners

Pairs of children in scattered formation. Use only eight or ten pairs at a time if the class is large or the space small. One is the leader, while the other, with eyes closed, is the follower. The leader continuously or intermittently whispers his partner's name, moving backward around the room. The follower uses this auditory clue as his direction, and goes where he is led. The leader has to accept responsibility for keeping his partner away from obstacles and other players. After a short time, change roles and/or partners.

Variation: Partners may be led by the sounds of small percussion instruments played very softly. Choose those with clearly distinctive timbres: one each from the four "families" (wood, metal, skin, rattles), such as sticks, triangle, drum, and maracas. Home made or improvised instruments like keys, a box of paper clips or two spoons are useful too.

Children and teacher investigate together all the acoustical properties of the various percussion instruments available.

For example, with a drum:
Discuss how and of what it was made. What other kinds do the children know about, or have seen and heard? Explore the sounds made by striking the drum in various places (rim, center, frame, underside) with the hands, fingers, thumbs, elbow. Try various types of mallets, felt head, rubber head, snare sticks, or woolly tympani mallets.

A hand drum (tambour) may be passed around a circle, with each child playing it in his own way while the others listen. Stress the importance of striking carefully, cleanly and with rebound to produce musical sounds and not damage the drum. When the different sounds are familiar, the children can close their eyes while the teacher plays, briefly. They then try to guess where and how, or with what, the sound was made.

All the other small percussion instruments can be explored in the same way.

Sleeping Beauty

There was a love-ly prin-cess, a prin-cess, a prin-cess, There was a love-ly prin-cess, Long time a-go.

"Sleep - ing Beau - ty" etc.

Instruments

Fairy tale adaptable for dramatic play, pantomime, puppets, or a singing game with percussion instruments.

In consultation with the children, instruments are chosen as sound identification of the characters, or to "illuminate" the action; a triangle for the princess, drum for the witch and perhaps coconut shells as the prince rides up. These can be played as introductions to the verses, or to accompany the singing. These sounds, however, may not necessarily keep a pulse, but may serve as a very free sound "picture". Sometimes the whole story could be told entirely without words.

These are typical verses, but others can be improvised to involve every child. Add a King and Queen, guards, etc. All verses follow the same pattern of repeated words (underlined).

1.   There was a lovely princess . . . Long time ago.
2.   She lived up in the tower . . . (atop a table?)
3.   An old witch came to see her . . .
4.   She made her stick her finger . . .
5.   The princess fell asleep . . . (add verses as they all fall asleep.)
6.   The hedges grew around them . . . (circle of surrounding children rises slowly)
7.   A handsome prince came riding . . . (from the hall)
8.   He cut down all the hedges . . . (tap shoulders, they fall)
9.   He woke the sleeping princess . . . (and additional characters)
10.   They had a happy wedding . . . (clapping or improvised dance)

Many adaptations are possible to suit time and space and abilities of children.

Three or four children stand before the class, each with a different, contrasting sounding percussion instrument. On a signal from the teacher, they are all struck simultaneously, one time, and the sound is allowed to fade completely. "Which could be heard the longest?"

Several combinations of instruments can be explored, with new children playing each time. The effectiveness of this listening and focusing exercise will be increased noticeably if the class keeps its eyes closed while the instruments are sounding.

Several children choose instruments and stand in a row facing the class. Each plays in turn, waiting until the previous sound has faded completely before striking his own instrument.

Alter the sequence and help the children notice the changes in the composition. Substitute other children, other instruments. Let the class decide on a pleasing sequence, and note (or even draw!) it, or tape-record it for future listening, or further explorations and additions.

The children can explore such sounds as a means of telling a story without words, or for dramatic effects to suggest a scenario for Hallowe'en, Christmas or other holiday. The familiar nursery rhymes, stories and fairy tales can be told, using only percussion instruments, and/or the sounds made with hands, feet and lips.

DYNAMICS

LOUD/SOFT
GETTING LOUDER - CRESCENDO
GETTING SOFTER - DECRESCENDO

- to distinguish between, and react to, loud and soft sounds.
- to produce loud and soft sounds, and make gradual changes in volume
- to use what has been learned in songs, rhymes, jingles and original compositions

The children move at random as the teacher plays a drum. When the sound is soft, they tiptoe, and when it shifts to loud, they stamp or otherwise match the sound with their bodies. The children can take turns conducting with the drum.

The teacher plays a drum, gradually varying the dynamic levels. A circle of children responds by moving closer in to the center as the sound gets softer (smaller) and widening out as the sound gets louder (bigger).

Another time, try the opposite reaction: tiptoe out toward the walls as the sound gets softer, and come stamping into the center of the room as the drum gets louder and more concentrated. Slightly older children who have seen or played with pebbles dropped in a pond will understand this variation.

Class and teacher sit together in a circle. With eyes closed, the children listen as the teacher claps a short rhythmic pattern of loud and soft beats, such as: loud loud soft soft loud The children imitate it immediately, together; later, a few at a time, and eventually, individually.

Variation: The pattern is presented, and the children try to pass it intact around the circle. Should the echo "fall apart" a new pattern can be given to the child who missed, letting him be the first to pass it on. Some children can remember and reproduce the original pattern even when their neighbor has given it incorrectly.

Eventually, a longer pattern can be tried:

soft   soft   soft loud soft loud soft loud

Grizzly Bear

A. Griz - zly bear, a griz - zly bear is sleep - ing in a cave.

B. Please be ver - y qui - et, ver - y, ver - y qui - et,

C. If you wake him, if you shake him, he gets ver - y MAD!

**soft
loud**

Begin with one bear asleep in the center of a circle. Holding hands and singing in full voice, the circle moves to the right during "A" and its repeat. During "B", they drop hands, turn around, and make exaggerated tiptoe, finger-to-lips motions, singing extremely softly, and walking in single file, clockwise.

Still singing softly, they take a few steps to the center during the first two measures of "C", and step backward on the last two measures. A natural crescendo takes place here, as the bear awakens and begins to chase someone at the word "MAD". Should he catch someone before the wall can be touched for "safe", the one who was caught joins him as a second bear the next time.

Should the cumulative effect prove too exciting, have the captured one change places with the bear.

Very young children may omit the steps to the center, and just keep tiptoeing until it is time to scatter or be caught.

Playing outdoors, some typical magic "safe" can be devised; stooping, touching wood, or a tree or fence.

One child goes out of the room, and a small object is hidden. He is called back in, and his classmates guide him to the object with handclaps. When he is close to it, they clap louder; as he moves farther away, they clap more and more softly. Sudden movement from the seeker may bring sudden change in the dynamic level of the clapping.

Variation: The same game can be accompanied with a simple, familiar song or nursery rhyme, sung softly or loudly as described above. This is the same as the children's game of "Hot and Cold".

A semi-circle of children, each with a percussion instrument. Class and teacher first explore ways of indicating whether to play softly or loudly; hand or arm gestures, strong or weak movement, etc. Then a child faces the group and conducts it any way he likes.

Variation: After some investigation of which instruments sound best played loudly or softly, the group divides according to these qualities and the conductor can bring them in alternately as he chooses. The end results may be very free and non-metric, or may produce strict rhythmic patterns, according to the capacity and experience of the leader.

Teacher and class explore the sound qualities of the various instruments in the classroom, both traditional and improvised. Which ones have a sound of short duration? Which ones reverberate for a long time after being struck? Does the material of which it is made have anything to do with the sound length?

The Wolf

Melody: Hungarian

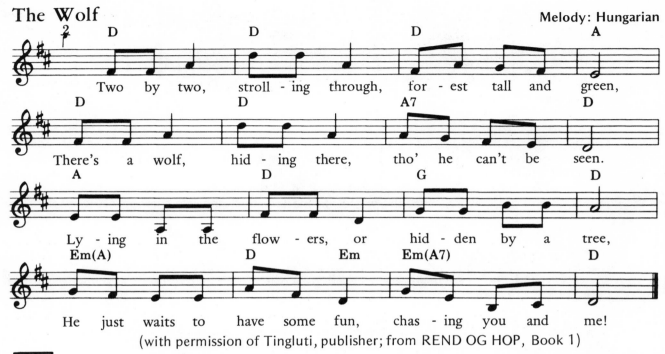

Two by two, stroll - ing through, for - est tall and green,

There's a wolf, hid - ing there, tho' he can't be seen.

Ly - ing in the flow - ers, or hid - den by a tree,

He just waits to have some fun, chas - ing you and me!

(with permission of Tingluti, publisher; from REND OG HOP, Book 1)

Circle of partners, facing counter-clockwise, inside hands joined. One child in the center is the wolf.

Keeping a little more than arm's length from the pair in front, the partners take seven steps, jauntily, following the beat, and perhaps swinging arms. On the last beat of the first line, they turn around, facing clockwise, and walk and sing the second line as the first.

On the last beat, they stand side by side, facing into the center.

Third line: take three or four steps into the center, and three or four steps out again.

Fourth line: repeat, scattering at the end, as the wolf tries to catch someone.

The wolf and his new partner take their places in the circle of partners as the game begins again, and the one left without a partner is the new wolf.

N.B. Should the class have an even number of children, the teacher plays too, thus assuring a "lone wolf" every time.

Variation: To simplify for younger children, let the partners walk anywhere in the room, perhaps changing direction at the end of each line.

The children and teacher recall and/or learn rhymes, jingles and short poems whose "dramatic" content lends itself to experiments with dynamic effects. The whole group, (and later several small groups) will enjoy "Sing a Song of Sixpence" or "Humpty Dumpty" or some of the colorful poems of David McCord, Maurice Sendak and Eleanor Farjean.

Explore the children's suggestions for making these dynamic changes visual. Try to find graphic representation for getting louder, suddenly softer, very loud, level of ordinary speech, etc. Some typical suggestions: writing with a different color, thick and thin lines, large shapes getting smaller, etc. Should the class come up with something close to the traditional signs ⟨ and ⟩, by all means tell them the names crescendo and decrescendo, and that these are known all over the world, no matter what language the musicians speak. They love to say the big words.

Teacher and class can make a composition, based on a short story in a book, or entirely original, putting short sentences on the board with their dynamic variations graphically marked.

It can be performed by small groups for the rest of the class, told in assembly, or taped for future enjoyment and exploration. Very often the children's work is completely abstract, but another time they may invent an entire scenario.

Example: Sun shines, child and dog walk in the park, clouds form, lightning and thunder, rain getting stronger, child and dog seek shelter, rain slows, drips, sun appears, child and dog go home, whistling.

PULSE

SIMULTANEITY
PULSE
TEMPO

— to lead as well as follow in group activities
— to understand and be able to reproduce regularly recurring sounds (pulse) to various tempi
— to experience the unifying effects of group speaking, singing, and playing

The teacher begins by pantomiming a familiar, recognizable action, such as washing and drying hands, hammering a nail, sewing, sawing, painting, etc. The class guesses and verbally describes what it saw. Very soon, the children will want to try this miming themselves, thus building a repertoire for later improvisation in other games.

Variation: Pairs of children can work for an alloted amount of time in various places in and out of the room, coming together at the end to share what they have evolved . . . poem, short story, ball game, circus. There are many possibilities here for coordination with other curricula.

Using the melody and words to "As I Went Over Sea and Land" (page 35), play this game: One child in the middle of a circle improvises an action such as hopping, turning, creeping, while the class sings the song. When they reach the line, "My home is in . . . . . land", they insert the name of his action. On the last line, he chooses someone to take his place.

Variation: The circle moves to the right, slowly, while the "old man" in the center, goes left. At the word, "homeland", he stops in front of a "traveler", who steps to the center and improvises a movement for all to imitate until the end of the verse. Traveler becomes the next old man.

Around the Moon

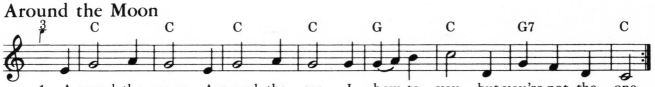

1. A-round the moon, A-round the sun, I bow to you, but you're not the one.
2. I ask you please, To dance with me, So say you'll try, and not say good - bye.

**improvisation
imitation**

Two concentric circles, with an equal number in each: inside circle faces out. The circles move slowly in opposite directions, singing the first verse. By the end of the verse, each child should be directly in front of someone in the other circle. (In the beginning it may take some of the second verse to get this straight.) The second verse is sung standing still. Then the following tune which may be played instrumentally on recorder or piano at first, is sung while those in one circle improvise a movement and the partner in the other circle imitates it. A drum beat, softly played by the teacher, may encourage more "dancey" movements. (Note the change of meter in the next tune.)

I Like to Dance With You

Oh, I like to dance with you. Can you do just what I do? La

la la. la la la, la la, la la la, la la la la la la la!

The two circles take turns being the leader and imitator. (The circles can be formed quickly by having the children "count off" by two's and then letting the 1's or 2's step to the center and form their own circle, facing out.)

Simplify the game for younger children by having one or the other circle stand still and clap during the first verse. This will enable those moving to find a partner more easily. The teacher should stand by, ready to help in securing partners.

Short lines of four or five children. The head of each line initiates a rhythmic movement which the others imitate. Change leaders on a signal. Like "Follow the Leader", there is no instrumental accompaniment here; rather, let each line find and keep its own pulse.

Several small circles, no more than five to seven children in each, scattered all over the space. The members of each circle decide among themselves who shall be first, second, and so on. One after the other, they improvise a movement for the rest to imitate. Although the teacher can signal for a change to the next one at first, the children can very soon control how long each one is in the center.

Suggest that the leader might go back into the circle as soon as all the others are doing the movement to his satisfaction. Eventually this can be done to piano or a recording of folk-dance music, or carefully selected pop music instrumentals with a swinging beat.

Pairs of children, facing, scattered anywhere in the room. One begins as leader, and both close their eyes, touching only the palms of their hands together. The leader makes slow, gentle and sustained movements; his partner follows. Exchange leaders, then partners. This can be done sitting or standing, but silently.

The teacher can help the concentration by creating an "atmosphere" with soft, freely improvised sounds on long-sounding metal instruments.

Variation: The same minimal contact is maintained, but the leader has his eyes open and guides his "blind" partner around the room.

Pairs, each in a good space. Children face each other, prepared to take turns as leader. First one takes up a pose and holds it, like a statue. The other immediately takes the same pose in mirror image. It may help to have young children begin with arms and head only.

As I Went Over Sea and Land

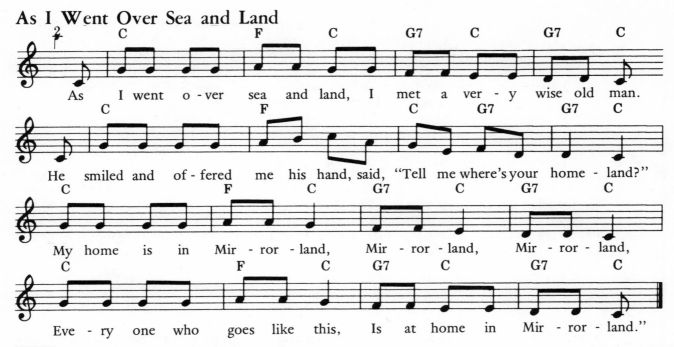

As I went o-ver sea and land, I met a ver-y wise old man.

He smiled and of-fered me his hand, said, "Tell me where's your home-land?"

My home is in Mir-ror-land, Mir-ror-land, Mir-ror-land,

Eve-ry one who goes like this, Is at home in Mir-ror-land."

**improvisation
imitation**

Three different movement patterns appear in this game: a circle, partners, and random movement.

During the singing of the first two lines of the song, the circle walks slowly to the right. By the end of the second line, each child turns to someone near him, shakes hands and faces him as a partner. They sing the last two lines, one initiating some action for the other to mirror exactly. (Suggest slow, gradual and sustained gestures.)

When the song has ended, the class moves at random, waiting for a signal, such as a triangle chime, to reform the circle.

Variation: The teacher can improvise on recorder, piano or drum while the children move at random. Their musical sense can be aided by making this improvisation the same length (four phrases as the song. The end of this instrumental interlude can be the signal for the circle to form.

Variation: For younger children, let exactly one-half of the class be the "wise old man", and stand or sit still while the rest go "travelling". In this case, the travelers should stop and shake hands with a chosen partner at the end of the first line. Exchange groups.

As an extension or later variation of the echo/mirror exercise on Page 34, the children try to keep a continuous and simultaneous flow of movements, mirroring each other exactly. This requires more concentration than standing still and waiting for the pose to be complete before assuming the same shape. Change partners often so that the children become familiar with each others' way of moving. Change leaders on signal. "Help your partner by keeping your eye on each other. Move so slowly that I cannot tell who is leading."

The teacher is in the center of a circle, where all can see. She then "falls forward", catching her balance with one foot forward. The children imitate this step, attempting to put the foot down at _exactly_ the same moment as the teacher. This is repeated several times, changing feet and facing direction. Eventually, the foot placement can follow a regular rhythmic pulse. The goal here is muscle control as well as simultaneity.

The children move freely at random, each walking his own pace. The teacher calls the name of one child, and the rest notice his walking pace and try to follow it.

Variation: The one whose name is called, continues his pace, but claps the rhythm of his steps. Later, the child may be chosen by handing her an instrument to play as she steps. Try to encourage the use of the whole space, rather than falling into an endless circling, as children will.

A pulse is played on a drum for the class to walk to. (Eventually a child can do this.) Extend this by having the class try to continue in the same pulse even when the drum has stopped. Change the speed slightly each time the drum begins anew.

Doctor Katchel

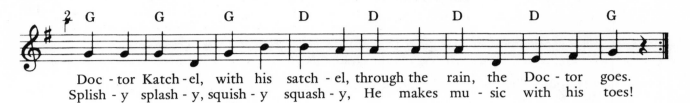

Doc - tor Katch - el, with his satch - el, through the rain, the Doc - tor goes.
Splish - y splash - y, squish - y squash - y, He makes mu - sic with his toes!

Possible Xylophone Part

 The circle represents the many places the doctor must visit on his rounds. The teacher and (later a child) walks around the inside, and the class accompanies his steps with a "wet" sounding clap (only two or three fingers slapped softly on the opposite palm.) At the end of the song, the doctor stops in front of someone (the patient), who continues to clap the same pulse, alone and without singing. This means the child must retain and internalize and repeat what has just been heard and seen. The patient who can accurately keep the pulse can be the doctor next time.

The doctor is advised to change the pulse (hurrying to get there, tired at the end of the day, walking briskly in the rain, etc.) to re-focus the children's attention on the pulse.

Moving at random to the teacher's drum or tambourine pulse, the class tries to stop precisely when the drum stops. Anyone who falters, takes extra steps or loses balance, joins the rhythm player and helps by hand-clapping.

In the beginning, it may help to end with two stronger beats as a clue. Playing two or four simple, clear phrases will sharpen the children's awareness, too.

Variation: Two groups of children: One group establishes a pulse and plays it with hands or feet, to which the other group moves. Signal for a change of roles.

A circle of children claps a pulse initiated at first by the teacher. A child steps into the center and tries to find a way of moving that fits the pulse as given, such as hopping, sliding, jumping. Whenever he likes, he calls another to take his place. The teacher can vary the pulse often, making it soft, slow and strong, or uneven.

Variation: One or two lines or snakes of children, whose leader determines the pulse and the manner of moving, as well as the direction, are formed. On a sound signal, the leader goes to the end of the line, and the next child has a chance to lead.

Sewing Needle

Sew, sew, sew - ing nee - dle, sew, sew, sew - ing nee - dle, sew, sew, etc.

A line of children, with the "needle" or leader at one end, and the "knot" or anchor at the other. The "knot" places one hand (e.g. the left) firmly against the wall, piano or other stable object, and keeps it there throughout the game. (Choose the tallest child for this.) The sewing "needle" leads the whole line, hands joined, under the arch made by the last child and the wall. Move slowly, in pulse with the song. When the whole line has been pulled through, the "knot" will finish with his arms crossed in front of him, and he will be facing in the opposite direction. The next time around, the leader takes the line under the arch made by the "knot" and the next-to-last child, and this one, too, will end up facing in the opposite direction.

Children must be reminded <u>not</u> to go under their own arms, but to cross them in front of the body, to complete a "stitch". It will help to put them in the finished position, before they sing and play, so that they can see the eventual outcome of this winding-up motion. To do this have each child in a side-by-side line of children cross their right arms over their left and join hands in this way.

The game can end when all have been "stitched", or (for older or more experienced children) they can reverse and "pull out the basting thread". To do this, the needle must move backward, through the same "holes" he went into before, thereby untwisting everybody's arms as he goes.

This is easiest when those standing in line, arms crossed, give a little tug on the hand of the child being "unstitched" and rather pull him through.

Now take out the bast-ing stitch-es

The class divides into two lines or snakes, facing forward. Each one represents a kind of train; one is the slow freight train, the other the faster express train. Using a felt-headed mallet, the teacher plays one of these pulses on a drum, thus signalling that train to move, following its leader (engineer). When the drumbeats alternate, the first group stops, and a new engineer moves up, while the previous one becomes the "caboose". The second train begins to move, walking or shuffling as soon as it hears its own beat on the drum.

Standing still in scattered formation, the children and teacher decide on a certain number of drumbeats, for example, seven drumbeats. These are played steadily by the teacher, with the children counting them aloud. The drum stops, but the children, without any pause, begin to walk the same number of steps, keeping the pulse exactly. They stop after seven steps and listen as the drum begins again, perhaps this time in a new tempo, a little faster or slower. Try this with any number of pre-arranged beats from 3 to 12.

Down By the Station

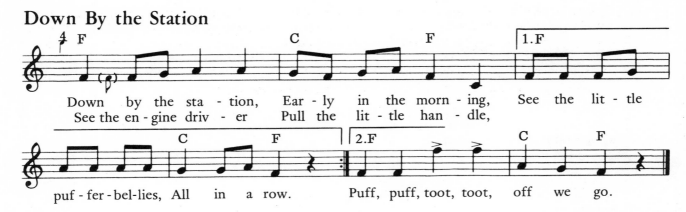

Down   by the sta - tion,   Ear - ly   in the morn - ing,   See   the   lit - tle
See the en - gine driv - er   Pull the   lit - tle   han - dle,

puf - fer - bel - lies, All   in   a   row.   Puff, puff, toot, toot,   off   we   go.

**getting
gradually
faster**

**gradually
slower**

**steady
tempo**

Teacher and children explore various ways to show and do slow clapping, that gradually increases in speed, such as broad, open, round arm gestures, with the clap falling in a regular place. As the pulse gets faster, the space occupied by the gesture will decrease, until it will be found necessary to clap quite close to the other hand for speed.

Sing the song a few times until it is familiar. Then the teacher, as "engineer", starts the very slowest handclaps, and the class, as the "cars", must follow the pace exactly. When an appropriate tempo is reached by the entire group, other train songs may be sung, using the clapping, or percussion instruments as accompaniment. Once the song ends, the "engineer" begins to bring the train into the station by gradually slowing the beat, with gestures getting larger and larger, and finally stopping. Eventually, let a child be "engineer".

This exercise makes considerable demands on the leader, because he must not only be able to do the changes in tempo smoothly and accurately, but must always be aware of the group's ability to follow his actions; his arm movements must be clearly defined and not exaggerated.

Train songs might include: "This Train is Bound for Glory"

"She'll be Comin' Round the Mountain"

"I've Been Workin' on the Railroad"

Seated in a circle with the teacher, each child says his name as he turns to look at his neighbor on the right. Eye-contact is maintained, but the pace may be entirely non-metric.

Variation: The next time, a small and distinct sound is passed around the circle, such as a tongue-click, knock on the floor, thigh-pat, finger-snap, two claps. Often, if each child has a percussion instrument, a regular rhythmic pulse may evolve.

With the teacher playing a soft and steady pulse on a drum, the class tries to pass such a pattern around right on the beat. Making the pattern two or three beats long will give young children more time to react.

Small percussion instruments, real or improvised, are dispersed widely over the floor. Following a steady pulse beat played by the teacher, the children move freely but carefully among them. When the drum stops, each child stops next to an instrument and either picks it up, or sits down and holds it. A familiar song is sung, and the children accompany it on the instruments as they sing. If there are not enough instruments, the extra children can clap. At the end of the song, the instruments are put down on the floor and the class moves again to the drum beat.

Some children will accompany a 4/4 song with ♩ ♩ , others with ♩♩♩♩ and some may simply follow the rhythm of the words. All are "correct", and should be allowed without comment. More experienced children will enjoy having the various metric ways pointed out to them, so they can experiment and choose a personal mode.

Choosing who will be "it" for any game can be an interesting exercise in playing pulse. The entire class can accompany the counting-out rhyme with claps on the accents, or only at the end. (See next pages.)

Examples of counting-out rhymes

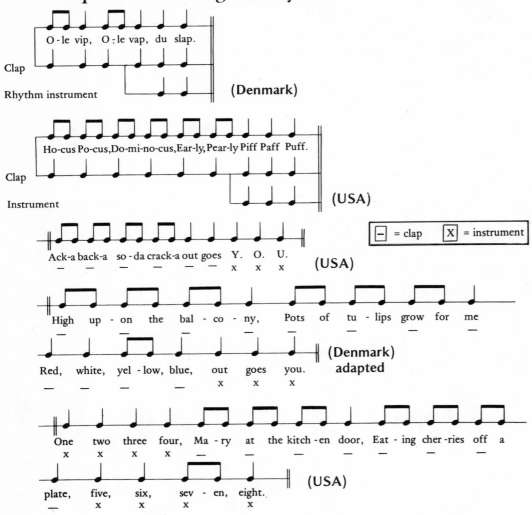

O - le vip, O - le vap, du slap.

Clap

Rhythm instrument (Denmark)

Ho-cus Po-cus, Do-mi-no-cus, Ear-ly, Pear-ly Piff Paff Puff.

Clap

Instrument (USA)

Ack-a back-a so - da crack-a out goes Y. O. U.
— — — — x x x (USA)

High up - on the bal - co - ny, Pots of tu - lips grow for me

Red, white, yel - low, blue, out goes you. (Denmark) adapted
— — — — x x x

One two three four, Ma - ry at the kitch -en door, Eat - ing cher -ries off a
x x x x — — — — — —

plate, five, six, sev - en, eight. (USA)
— x x x x

|−| = clap |X| = instrument

Some traditional rhymes for pulse exercises with clapping and/or instruments

Inky dinkey donkey,
Daddy bought a monkey
Monkey died, Daddy cried,
Inky dinkey donkey.

One potato, two potato,
Three potato, four,
Five potato, six potato,
Sev'n potato, MORE!

Wire, briar, limber lock,
Twelve geese in a flock,
One flew east, one flew west,
One flew over the cuckoo's nest.

Tinker, tailor, soldier, sailor
Rich man, poor man, beggerman, thief,
Doctor, lawyer, Indian chief.

Unguy, munguy, chicka-chicka-chunguy (pronounced ung-eye)
Alligator, unguy, o - - - ver.

Collect others from the children.

PITCH

HIGH-LOW
MOVING UP, DOWN
STEADY AND CONTINUOUS PITCH

— to distinguish between high and low tones separated by smaller and smaller intervals
— to understand, and be able to reproduce accurately, stepwise melodic sequences, in progressively shorter series
— to use a corresponding terminology

 The teacher stands at the piano so that the children cannot see her hands. She strikes the highest, then the lowest note and asks if the children can tell which was the bird high in the air, and which one was the cow lying in the field.

Variation: The class points up or down as a high or low note is struck. The interval between the notes can be gradually diminished. Soon the class can be introduced to the same kinds of intervals on instruments of narrower range, such as the recorder or xylophone.

 Class moves at random as the teacher improvises. When high notes are heard, arms can go up, and the children dance on tiptoe (birds). Low notes are shown by crawling close to the floor or duck-walking, holding onto ankles. Let the children invent their own ways of moving.

 Two groups are formed one to react to the high, the other to the low tones played by the teacher. As long as either group hears its own pitch-range being played, it moves at random around the room, stopping short when the pitch changes so the opposite group can begin.

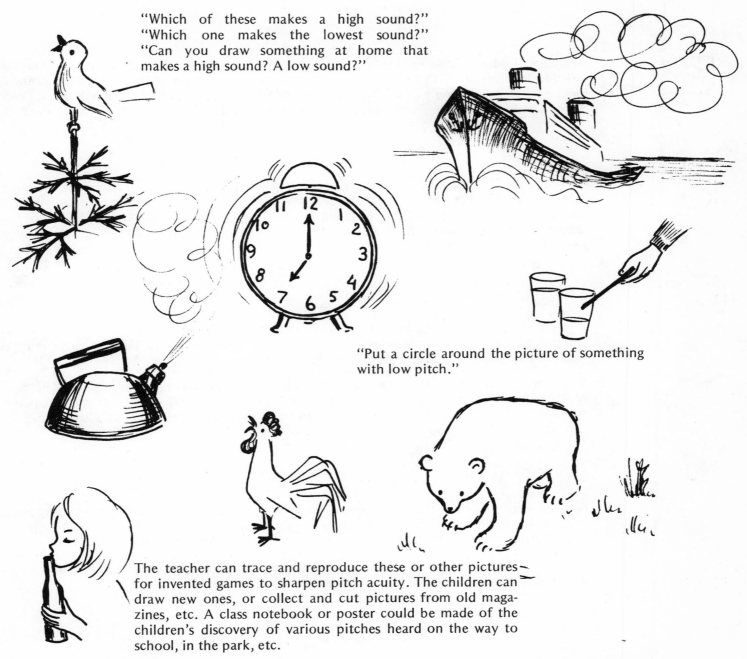

"Which of these makes a high sound?"
"Which one makes the lowest sound?"
"Can you draw something at home that makes a high sound? A low sound?"

"Put a circle around the picture of something with low pitch."

The teacher can trace and reproduce these or other pictures for invented games to sharpen pitch acuity. The children can draw new ones, or collect and cut pictures from old magazines, etc. A class notebook or poster could be made of the children's discovery of various pitches heard on the way to school, in the park, etc.

With the children sitting evenly distributed on the floor, single tones are sung or played on a melody instrument. With their bodies, the children react to high or low tones by reaching up on tiptoe, or squatting quickly to the floor. Initially, this should be done with eyes closed, to insure that each child is responding individually, and not imitating what he sees others do.

One or more children sit in the center of a circle with a pile of blocks, small boxes or a stacking toy. The teacher (or a child) strikes high or low-pitched tones on a melody instrument, pausing after each one. A block is added to the "tower" when a high tone is heard, and removed when a low tone is heard. Alternate children often, encouraging those who are waiting to observe carefully for practice.

A piece of thick yarn or a jump rope is held stretched out between two children, who must react to the high or low tones played by moving the rope up or down. The rest of the children walk under the high tones and jump over the low ones.

Variation: The rope is tied to two stationery objects, such as sturdy chairs, about a half meter or 18 inches from the floor. A line of children shows with its bodies whether the tone played was high or low: after a high tone, a few can jump over the rope, and after a low tone, a few can wriggle under the rope.

Four children at a time play this game. Three chairs are placed far apart in the room, and a child stands beside each. The fourth child plays high or low tones, slowly, on a melody instrument. "High" is shown by standing on the chair, "low" by squatting beside it.

Variation: When most of the children can do this easily, an intermediate tone can be introduced, indicated by sitting in the chair. Call this "middle" pitch.

Two Cats

Two cats went climb - ing up a tree, krit - te - vit - te vit bom bom,
And they were play - ing games you see, krit - te - vit - te vit bom bom.

Said one, now lis - ten here, my friend, krit - te - vit - te - vit - te - vit - te - vit bom bom,

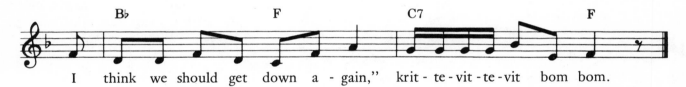

I think we should get down a - gain," krit - te - vit - te - vit bom bom.

High - low

Sing the song a few times until it is familiar. (If "kritivitte" is too difficult, find other nonsense syllables the children like and can do.)

After the first verse is sung, a child tries to play two tones on a melody instrument that show aurally what the cats did, such as a high tone, then a low tone if they came down, or the reverse if they went up.

Repeat after the second verse. It may help in the beginning to use only two tone-blocks, an octave apart, or to place only two such bars on the metallophone.

Variation: Out of the sight of the class, the teacher plays one of the pairs of notes, low-high or high-low, and the children try to say where the cats are going this time.

Verse 2.

They scrambled down and took a rest, Kritte . . .
The other said, "No, UP is best," Kritte . . .
So they climbed up that tree again, Kritte . . .
And that's a game that has no end, Kritte . . .

Pitch differences may be easily explored through the use of familiar stories and fairy tales. There are many, like the "Three Bears", "Red Riding Hood" and the "Billy Goats Gruff", where three distinct voice ranges are needed to be effective in dramatic play. The children can speak the dialogue in the proper pitch as the teacher pauses in the story telling, or they may act out the whole story themselves. Find other stores or poems with the magic number "3", and/or a set of small, medium and large characters.

More experienced children enjoy dividing into groups of four to six, going off for a prescribed length of time to work out the playlet, and returning to share it with the others, either in pantomime or using the appropriate pitches.

Variation: As the teacher tells the story, three children, each with a tone block of low, medium or high pitch, accompany the dialogue.

A metallophone or alto glockenspiel is hung on the blackboard (use a screw-eye and cord) with only two bars in position, and a house is drawn next to it. Example A We imagine that a ball breaks one of the windows (a bar is struck) and the class tries to determine which window was "broken"; the high or the low one, and to cross it out, as indicated by the pitch.

Variation: Try playing the tone out of sight of the class.

Each child is given a duplicated sheet like Example B. Play the same game as above, with children crossing out or coloring windows at their seats. (Names or initials on the sheets will help in evaluating progress.) The intervals played can be gradually diminished.

When the two-pitch game is easily mastered, add a third, intermediate tone. The objective is the same, but the story can be varied: for instance, where the light goes on in the morning, or a friend is visiting, or where the mailman delivers a letter to an apartment. Example C shows a house with three floors.

The instrument may be safely propped on an orchestra music stand, and tilted and raised into clear sight of the class. Select an instrument whose sound continues long enough to help those who are unsure of pitch.

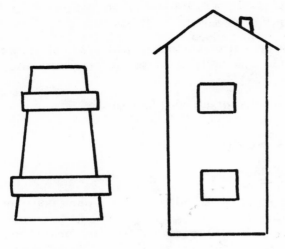

EXAMPLE A

EXAMPLE B

EXAMPLE C

The teacher plays a short pattern of high and low tones on an instrument, and then immediately draws a graphic representation of the pattern on the board: . . ▪ (low, low, high).

Extend this by letting two children be instrument player and "symbol drawer". Alternate often, until most of the class can do this easily. Reverse the procedure also, drawing the symbol first, and having a child play it.

Variation: Each child, with pencil and paper, draws what he hears.

As part of a seated circle, the teacher plays an ascending, stepwise phrase on a melody instrument, and the children respond by rising slowly to standing position. Reverse the movement while a descending phrase is played. Association made with the sun, or rockets, or even the children themselves, morning and evening, will help.

Variation: The arms alone may be used. The children take turns in directing the action by playing the music on xylophone or melody bells.

The song on the next page, "Come and Sing Your Name for Me" may be used again with more experienced children in another way. While the class sings the song, (perhaps changing the words to "play your name") the teacher taps one of the children, who then goes to the instrument and plays his name on "g" and "e". The class echoes, singing.

This exercise can lead directly to the study of musical notation, first in the form of round note heads (mallet heads, where they were played) on the bars of a metallophone drawing, as in Example A. Later, there can be two lines extended from the bars of the instrument itself, as it hangs on the board, and the two notes drawn on them, as in Example B.

Sing Your Name

Come and sing your name for me, Who will the first one be?
(play) (last)

Possible Xylophone Accompaniment etc.

metallophone

The song is sung by the class while the teacher, and later a child, plays the xylophone part to keep the pulse and reinforce pitch. The two single notes are played on a metallophone or tone blocks, and immediately afterward, four children sing their names consecutively. Hopefully, (but not necessarily) they will sing on the given interval, "g-e". In the middle of the game, a change to "next one" is possible. To end the game, or as it gets to the last few children, sing "last one"!

Variation: In a small group, or for more pitch practice, have only two children in a row sing their names. After each one does so, the class sings the names in echo fashion, attempting to maintain a smooth rhythmic flow.

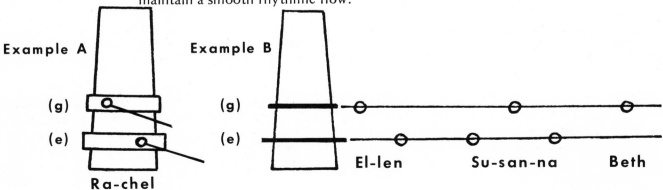

Example A

(g)
(e)

Ra-chel

Example B

(g)
(e)

El-len   Su-san-na   Beth

The teacher, while throwing a beanbag or soft, non-bouncing ball to one of the children, indicates vocally the path of a rocket, or shooting star. (Up, down, or straight ahead). The child who catches the ball tells aloud in what direction he heard the rocket travel, and becomes the next one to make the sound and throw the ball.

A crepe paper streamer about a yard or meter long with a small weight (pebble) wrapped and tied at one end, is an effective and visually delightful addition, especially if the game is played outdoors.

The teacher shows the rocket movement with voice and broad arm gestures that the class immediately imitates. The class can be divided into several groups, each one responsible for showing one specific direction. The task of conducting the groups may be alternated between the teacher and a child, even to indicating two directions at once!

Variation: A melodic passage or simple scale is played, and the class shows with arm movements, the direction it is going: up, down, level.

Can you show, with your voice and/or body, the way these things are moving?

The teacher sings a smooth melodic line, either a part of a familiar song, or improvised, at the same time drawing its contour on the blackboard.

Example: "Yankee Doodle" may look like this:

After some practice, the children can do this at their seats, singing and drawing simultaneously with crayon and paper.

Variations: The class sings one phrase at a time from a familiar song while one child at a time tries to draw it on the board.

Eventually, the children can work with partners; one sings while the other draws, and then changing places. This graphic visualization of melody is a useful introduction to sight singing and notation later on, because it accustoms the eye to see whole phrases rather than individual notes.

 Using a melody instrument to play short upward, downward or non-moving sequences of tones, the teacher conducts the childrens' pantomime: like firemen, they climb up the ladder, down the ladder or remain in place, "marking time". These are shown by holding imaginary ladder rungs in alternate hands as they step forward, (up) backward, (down) or in place.

 Short lines of players represent the hoses that the firemen at the head must carry up and down the ladders to put out a fire. Short scale passages are played to indicate where the firemen must go, and a single repeated tone pictures them level, as on a rooftop. Advise very careful movement backing down!

Variation: Three separate groups are formed, each to respond to a particular musical passage. Alternate leaders often.

RHYTHM

RHYTHM OF MOVEMENT
WORD RHYTHMS
MELODIC RHYTHM
IMPROVISATION

— to understand and reproduce short, recurrent rhythmic units
— to be able to create similar patterns
— to use such rhythms as an accompaniment to music

The teacher, and later a child, begins to walk in a steady rhythm, and the children clap an accompaniment to the steps. If he changes to a faster or slower pace, the clapping must adjust quickly to match it. The class will soon discover that the distance between the stepping feet and the clapping hands is exactly related, especially with slow steps.

Variation: Small percussion instruments, played softly, can accompany the steps. Rotate walkers (conductors!), players and clappers often until all are quite secure.

In conjunction with a zoo visit, or animal film, class and teacher discuss and explore the various ways in which animals move. Characteristic walks are tried: stiff legged giraffe; slow, heavy elephant; quick, light mouse; smooth, fluid tiger; etc. The teacher then whispers the name of an animal to each child in a circle. When his animal's name is called, the child walks around the inside of the circle and back to place, while the rest of the children clap the pulse of his steps. Later each child can choose an animal for himself, secretly, and there will be duplications. (Alternate fast and slow, heavy and light animals.)

Variation: Two lines are formed, one to imitate a slow animal, the other a fast one, letting the groups choose. Their movements are signalled with, perhaps, drum and woodblock, with each line stopping when it hears the opposite signal.

Can you imitate the way
these animals walk?
Can you clap the rhythm
of their steps?

In the center of a seated or standing circle of children, the teacher performs a regularly recurring pattern of fast and slow steps, pausing after each repetition.

Example:

♫ ♩ ♫ ♩ ♩ ♩

quick, quick, quick, quick, slow, slow

As soon as the children perceive the pattern, they clap in accompaniment.

Variation: When the teacher stops moving, the class tries to continue clapping the pattern alone. Eventually the children can invent these short patterns.

Using the tag-words of "walk" for ♩ and "run-ning" for ♫ , the teacher makes and moves in a short, continuous pattern. When the children discover the pattern, they join in, moving and speaking simultaneously. Let children try conducting.

Variation: Short lines of four or five children are formed. The leader improvises a pattern for the rest to follow, and all speak the tag words as they move around the room. On a signal, the leader goes to the end of the line and the next child begins with his own new pattern.

Frequent, continued experience with the whole group "run-ning" and doing the slower "walk" in alternation will reinforce this contrast. This helps the children control their movements more accurately and to feel the two rhythms with their own bodies.

In a circle, the teacher plays a pattern on the drum. The class tries to speak the pattern accurately, using tag-words.

Example:

♩ ♩ ♫ ♩

Walk walk run-ning walk

Adam's Seven Sons

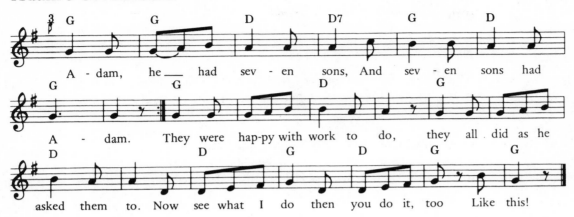

A - dam, he had sev - en sons, And sev - en sons had
A - dam. They were hap-py with work to do, they all did as he
asked them to. Now see what I do then you do it, too Like this!

improvisation

Two lines, facing each other down the length of the room. The lines may be called "A" and "B" if they consist of boys and girls interspersed, and one line may have small percussion instruments. While singing the first line, the "A" group walks forward eight steps (one step for each bar) and backward to place on the repeat. The second line of the song is sung standing still. During the singing of the third line of the song, the first child in the "B" line steps out in front and center of the "A" line. When the song ends, she begins to do a short repeated pattern of ♩ and ♫ perhaps ♩ ♩ ♫ ♫

walk walk run-ning run-ning

imitation

As soon as those in the "A" line have perceived the pattern, they clap it or play it on the instruments they hold. When all seem to have grasped it, the leader skips back to place. Another two or three may try before the roles of the two lines are reversed and/or instruments exchanged.

If played with a girls' and boys' line, (not necessarily an equal number in each) change the words as the girls' line is moving:

Eve had se - - ven daugh - ters, and se - ven daugh-ters had Eve. etc.

With eyes closed and/or covered, the class sits in a circle. The teacher, and later a child, goes around the outside, moving in a clear pattern of walk, running, such as:

walk run-ning run-ning run-ning.

As soon as the children perceive the pattern, they accompany the steps with soft clapping, still without looking. In this way they must depend solely on auditory clues.

Each working in his own space, the children experiment freely with making individual walk-running patterns. From careful observation, the teacher will find a few who evolve clearly structured, steadily rhythmic foot patterns; she then calls one of these children by name. The class gives its attention to that child, who performs his pattern alone, and the rest imitate it as soon as they can.

A line of four or five children takes turns improvising and demonstrating patterns for the rest to imitate. The first one in the class to do this correctly joins the leading group, and gradually those who have had a turn sit down, to be replaced by new children. The patterns may also be played or clapped.

A category is chosen, such as trees, fruits, animals, cars, and the teacher says the names of several items in the category, clearly and rhythmically. Each word is repeated, and clapped according to its word-rhythm. The group then imitates, in pulse. An interesting pattern can evolve this way:

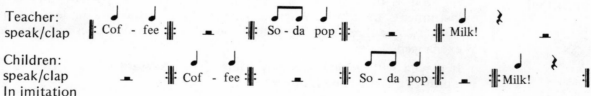

Teacher:
speak/clap

Children:
speak/clap
In imitation

Variation: After some experience with such echo games, the children can each take the name of one item in the category, and experiment with the order in which they stand and then speak their words, with the rest of the class echoing each time.

Old Dog, Full of Fleas

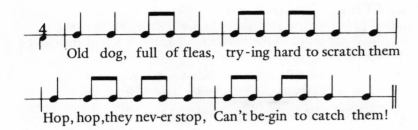

Old dog, full of fleas, try-ing hard to scratch them

Hop, hop, they nev-er stop, Can't be-gin to catch them!

This rhyme is to be used as the "A" section of a small A-B-A form, with the children's individual improvisations as the "B" sections.

Prepare for these by helping the children work out their own "hopping" patterns of walk-running steps, basing them on their names, or other short word-patterns.

"We're all fleas, and each one of us has his own way of hopping". Let the whole class experiment at the same time, despite the seeming chaos.

improvisation   When the teacher sees one child who seems to be maintaining a steady pattern, a triangle can signal for quiet. The teacher calls the name of the chosen child, and tells the class, "Let's see if we can catch this flea".

imitation   The class watches and listens while the soloist shows his pattern. As they perceive it, the class claps his pattern, and this constitutes "catching the flea".

On a signal, they stop and repeat the rhyme together, trying for a new improvisation each time it ends. Experiment with accompaniments for the rhyme: claps, snaps, instruments.

N.B. There is no "wrong" improvisation. Even a clear and steady ♩ ♩ pulse beat is fine if that is what a particular child can handle well. Also, the teacher may want to use an especially interesting pattern as a basis for her own melodic improvisation on recorder, as the class claps it.

The teacher says two children's names consecutively, in a clear rhythmic manner: Mi-chael, Mi-ri-am.

The children respond as a class by clapping the rhythm of the two names. (♩ ♩ | ♫ ♩)
Later a child can be originator.

Starting with her own name, the teacher says it, claps it and passes it on to the next child in a circle. Each child repeats the clapped pattern until it "comes home". Every child in the circle gets to send his own name around the circle. Should the pattern fall apart, a new name can be started at that point, or the original one spoken for a reminder.

A category is chosen in discussion with the class, and several items are explored by speaking and clapping their word-rhythms. For example, fruits: (Choose only two at first)

Tan - ge - rine;   Ap - ple;   Pine - ap - ple;   Plum;   Wa - ter - me - lon.

Half the class stands spread out in the room, with eyes tightly closed. The rest of the class moves around them. Each of the movers tiptoes up behind someone standing, and lightly taps out one of these rhythm patterns on a shoulder. If the one who was tapped recognizes which word it was, she turns around and whispers it. Eyes are closed, and the tapper moves on to try again. Exchange groups when all have had a turn, or let a correct answer be rewarded with a change of roles.

Variation: Those who are standing still hold small percussion instruments, (real or improvised) and then play the word-rhythm as they give their answers.

The same kind of game can be played in a circle. One child in the center is "it" and closes his eyes. Another comes up behind him and taps the word-rhythm, as above. If "it" answers correctly, he gets to choose the next tapper. From then on, every tapper becomes "it" for one turn. It may be wise to begin the game with the teacher as the first to be "it".

A category is chosen, discussed and explored. Then two items are combined to make an interesting pattern, and it is eventually performed by alternating stamping and clapping, or two other contrasting self-made sounds.

Example: clap

Daf - fo - dil

stamp

Dai - sy

Teachers will find a set of cards with categories and typical examples to be very useful for this and other games. Collect items with interesting, and contrasting, distinctive rhythmic patterns in broad categories such as cars, tools, sports teams, occupations, as well as the more familiar trees, flowers, birds and animals.

Texts for rhythmic speech and instrumental exploration

Other than names and simple word combinations as seen previously, many short sayings, proverbs and the children's own chants can provide unlimited opportunities for illustrating rhythmic speech. Transferring the patterns to clapping, snapping and stamping, or to the playing of percussion instruments will encourage improvisation with sound colors (e.g. wood, skin and metal) as accent and contrast. Each repetition can be another exploration of dynamics, solo and group work and orchestration.

Together, the teacher and the children can keep a collection of such short texts, in co-ordination with other parts of the curriculum, such as reading, spelling and creative writing.

Examples:

1. Cold hands, warm heart.
2. Better late than never. ♫ ♫ ♫ ♩ ‽
3. Don't count your chickens before they are hatched.
4. Something old, something new,
   Something borrowed, something blue.
5. Who's that . . . tapping at the window? ♩ ‽ ♩ ‽ | ♫ ♫ ♩ ♩
   Who's that . . . knocking at the door?
6. You buy milk, I'll buy flour, ♫ ♩ ♫ ♩
   We'll have pie in half an hour. ♫ ♫ ♫ ♩
7. All things come to him who waits. ¾ ♩ ♩|♩ ♩|♩ ♩|♩.

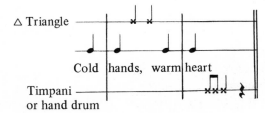

The following exercises, also found under other chapter headings, will sharpen the children's perception of rhythm patterns, and lead to the teacher's ability to invent new games according to the abilities of the class. Daily practice with such experiences will give the children confidence in improvising, and provide a firm basis for later work in musical activities.

1. The class echoes and repeats with clapping only, simple patterns performed by the teacher on an instrument, or walk-running, or tongue-clicks, without words.

2. As she claps or plays a pattern, the teacher makes and holds eye contact with the child who is to echo it. As soon as he has done so, he invents a new pattern, making eye contact with the child he wishes to have echo him. Try to maintain the rhythmic flow by avoiding long pauses due to the selection of an echo partner, or execution of a complicated pattern.

3. The teacher plays a repeated pattern of walk-running beats on a drum. As soon as they have grasped the pattern, the children join in by clapping and speaking the tag-words.

4. A melodic phrase is played on the piano, recorder or xylophone, and the children try to extract its rhythmic design by clapping as it is repeated.

5. The first line of a familiar song or nursery rhyme is played by the teacher on a drum, without speaking or singing, and the class echoes immediately by clapping or playing the rhythm of the words. It may be necessary to whisper the first few words as an aid to memory.

Variation: The word rhythms extracted from familiar rhymes and clapped or played by the children can provide the teacher with a basis for her own melodic improvisations on recorder or piano. The children can whisper or internalize the words as they clap or play.

Will You?

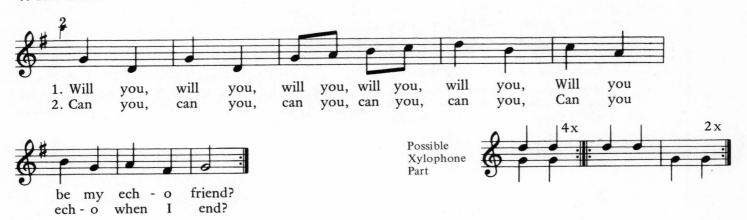

1. Will you, will you, will you, will you, will you, Will you
2. Can you, can you, can you, can you, can you, Can you

be my ech - o friend?
ech - o when I end?

Possible
Xylophone
Part

Contact

Imitation

Improvisation

In this echo exercise, the class and teacher are seated together in a circle. During the singing of the song, the teacher establishes eye contact with someone, and maintains it until the end of the song. This is the child chosen to echo.

The teacher claps a short rhythm pattern, perhaps only two measures long: ♩ ♫ | ♫ ♩ and the child imitates it to the best of his ability. If needed, the pattern is repeated or changed to suit the child.

The song is sung again, with the child who just echoed taking the role of the teacher, catching the eye of another during the song and inventing a pattern for him to imitate.

N.B. In the beginning, it is often difficult for children to devise clear, steady patterns of the proper length, or to imitate them accurately. No value judgment should be given, but the teacher will find this an indication that many other clapping and imitation exercises are needed to heighten the children's awareness. Their ability to structure and imitate develops very quickly through practice.

"Who knows a poem that begins with this rhythm?"

Teacher claps without saying the words. The children guess and imitate ("Deedle Deedle Dumpling"). "Hickory, Dickory Dock", "Mary Had a Little Lamb" and "Hot Cross Buns" are examples of others with distinctive opening lines. Some children may be more familiar with jump-rope rhymes or advertising jingles.

Playing the first line on a percussion instrument can act as an introduction to the singing of the song, or part of its pattern can be continued throughout as a rhythmic accompaniment to the song.

FORM

REPETITION
CONTRAST
A-A, A-B

— to perceive and understand short, regularly recurring phrases
— to detect elements of form in rhymes, jingles, songs and dances

Many of the exercises and songs in other parts of this book can provide additional material for an elementary understanding of form.

Standing anywhere in the room, the children listen to four steady pulsebeats played on a drum by the teacher. Without losing the pulse, they walk four steps in any direction and stop on the last beat. The teacher plays again, in the same pulse or a new one.

(Prepare for this by having the whole group walk to the drumbeats in various tempi, thereby learning muscle control as well as rhythmic accuracy.)

Variation: Short lines of four or five children, following the direction of the leader, listen and then move to the silent beat. Alternate leaders often, with the previous one going to the end of his line on a signal.

Using quick and slow beats, the teacher plays a short pattern for the children to translate into walking and running steps.

Example: Teacher plays:

Children move: run - ning,   run - ning,   walk,   walk.

Variation: Partners with inside hands joined or short lines as above, can move together, thus helping each other. After some experience with such activities, point out the two different parts of the form: listening/moving, or "A" and "B".

The Merry-go-round

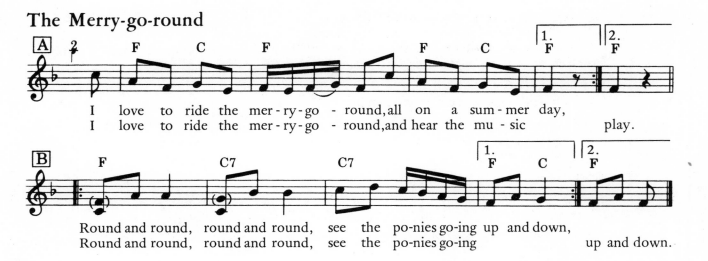

A I love to ride the mer-ry-go - round, all on a sum-mer day,
I love to ride the mer-ry-go - round, and hear the mu - sic play.

B Round and round, round and round, see the po-nies go-ing up and down,
Round and round, round and round, see the po-nies go-ing up and down.

Form: The melody has two sections, and each is repeated: A-A-B-B. The teacher can help the children invent a dance or game to accent the two parts of the melody.

Some suggestions:

1. Two circles, one inside the other, and walking slowly in opposite directions. At the end of "A" and its repeat, each child joins both hands with someone in the other circle. During "B", they can turn each other around, or go up and down alternately like a merry-go-round, or otherwise improvise.

2. A circle moves left for seven steps, using the eighth to change direction to the right on the repeat. Let the children improvise their own steps during "B".

3. Older children might like to take "scissors" steps to the left and right during "A", that is: step to the left with the left foot, bring the right up to close it and shift weight to the right foot. Do this eight times, then on the repeat, step to the right. Try a little skipping circle in place in "B".

4. Divide the class in half, and each half forms a line. One line will move during "A" with steady walking steps to ♩ ♩ ♩ ♩ and the other takes light running steps ♫ ♫ ♫ ♫ during "B". Change leaders at each repeat with the previous one going to the end of the line. Each line stands still until its own melody occurs in the singing.

Other suggestions to show form

5. Two groups are formed. One group plays the pulse of the A section on small instruments, such as sticks, while standing still. Meanwhile, the second group walks among a collection of instruments spread out on the floor, following the pulse: ♩ ♩ ♩ ♩ . When the A section ends, group one stops playing, and group two picks up the nearest instruments and accompanies the singing with eighth note beats: ♫ ♫ ♫ ♫ . The instruments are carefully replaced on the floor at the end of the song. Change the roles of the groups with each repeat.

Find other familiar folk, nursery or popular songs with two clearly distinctive parts, verse and chorus patterns, or solo-group dialogues, and explore their dance form possibilities.

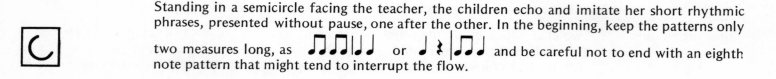

Standing in a semicircle facing the teacher, the children echo and imitate her short rhythmic phrases, presented without pause, one after the other. In the beginning, keep the patterns only two measures long, as ♫ ♫ ♩ ♩ or ♩ 𝄽 | ♫ ♩ and be careful not to end with an eighth note pattern that might tend to interrupt the flow.

Variation: Patterns may be made more interesting by changing the dynamic levels: loud, soft, gradually louder, etc.

A game of opposites may be played by having the class echo softly when the pattern is clapped loudly, and vice-versa. A gradual increase in volume might be answered with a gradual decrease, and so on. Naturally, this is more difficult.

The class sits in a circle, and tries to pass around a pattern initiated by the teacher. (see page 42) This time, however, the children try to "think" the pattern (internalize it) before clapping it.

Example:

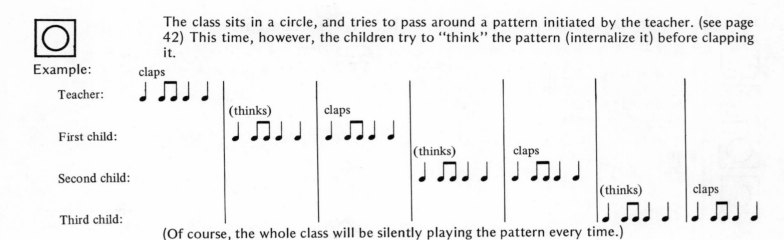

Teacher:

First child:

Second child:

Third child:

(Of course, the whole class will be silently playing the pattern every time.)

Alternation between groups or group and soloist

During the class' speaking of various rhymes and jingles, several groups can alternate according to the form-making divisions. Some rhymes lend themselves especially well to solo-tutti arrangements.

Example: Solo 1: A, B, C,

Solo 2: Tumbledown D,

Tutti: Cat's in the cupboard, and can't see me!

Such short rhymes offer many possibilities for play with dramatic contrast of vocal qualities; high, low, staccato, lyrical, and dynamic loud-soft changes.

In songs where there is built-in melodic, textual or rhythmic repetition, the sections may be said by a soloist the first time and a group the second. (e.g. "Hot Cross Buns"; "One, Two, Buckle My Shoe"; "Old MacDonald" and "Aunt Rhody" are examples of songs and rhymes that adapt easily to these arrangements.)

A good collection of folk songs and the children's own favorite rhymes will provide a rich source for speaking and singing games, as well as for composed dance forms.

Key to Diagrams

 Scattered, standing still

 Scattered formation in random movement

 Circle or ring

 Semi-circle

 Several small circles

 Line or "snake"

 Several short lines

 Pairs or partners

 Circle of partners or double circle

 A dot indicates one person in the center or leading

 Two lines, facing

Key to Instruments

 tom tom

 hand drum

 tambourine

 sleigh bells

 triangle

 cymbal

 claves

 wood block

 maracas

 finger cymbals

74

INDEX